Hemlock and Honey

by

Margaret Royall

First published 2025 by The Hedgehog Poetry Press,

5 Coppack House, Churchill Avenue, Clevedon. BS21 6QW

www.hedgehogpress.co.uk

Copyright © Margaret Royall 2025

The right of Margaret Royall to be identified as the author of this work has been asserted in accordance with the Copyright, Designs and Patents Act 1988. All rights reserved. No part of this publication may be reproduced, stored in or introduced into a retrieval system, or transmitted in any form, or by any means (electronic, mechanical, photocopying, recording or otherwise) without prior written permissions of the publisher. Any person who does any unauthorised act in relation to this publication may be liable for criminal prosecution and civil claims for damages.

ISBN: 978-1-916830-54-7

In Memory of Steve Cawte,
former editor of Impspired Magazine
to whom I owe a debt of gratitude

INTRODUCTION TO HEMLOCK & HONEY

a personal statement

As I approach my three score years and ten I have been thinking back over the past decades and analysing the memorable events that stand out for me most, reflecting on those that have exerted the greatest influence on my life. Indeed, there have been traumatic times, when life was turned upside down and huge changes were forced upon me. On the other hand I now understand, with the benefit of hindsight, that these have encouraged positive changes and led to hobbies, interests and new friendships that have greatly enriched my life. Without the trauma there could not be the rapture! In these poems I have therefore tried to explore both facets of life. Part One details the negatives and Part Two the positives, thus aiming to provide a balanced overview. I do not seek the sympathy card or see myself as a victim, nor do I want to suggest that life now is totally perfect. It's a case of moderation in all things.

I have chosen the sonnet form in many poems, having always enjoyed writing in form and particularly using sonnets. Recently I took a course with distinguished poet Anna Saunders on writing sonnets for contemporary times, which I greatly enjoyed. This then naturally followed through into my latest work. It has been a huge challenge to write in this concise poetic form that uses rhyme, but to do it in a non-intrusive way. I hope that in some small way I have succeeded and brought the reader with me on my journey. My wish is to demonstrate that despite life throwing us curve balls, with patient determination we can find solutions, coping strategies that enable us to emerge as stronger, more hopeful and better human-beings.

Margaret Royall

Contents

Introduction to Hemlock & Honey 3

Part One: Hemlock 9

Stigmata - a curse for ordinary mortals too 11
The first hard knock 12
Death at Halloween 13
Engulfed in darkness 14
Drowning 15
Ugly 16
A life-changing diagnosis 17
Friendship at crisis point 18
A map unleashes an unexpected response 20
Hope hidden in Pandora's Jar 21
How (not) to dress for a Birthday 22
Becoming Eve 23
When Gaia weeps 24
Psychosis 25
Hope denied 26
Time travelling with skylarks 27

Part Two: Honey 29

Aubade – dum vita est, spes est* 31
Life's natural rhythms 32
Expect the unexpected 33
Hide and Seek (*a metaphor for life's thrills and spills*) 34
Summer's last dance 35
River Mother 36
Evening on the Norfolk coast 37
This is enough for me 38
Monet Pursues His Obsession with Water Lilies 39
Zoomorphic* Talisman 40
A hopeless fashion addict reflects on recycling 41
The comforting rituals of life in a small country village 42
An unexpected visitation 43
Hemlock and Honey 44
Acknowledgment 46

Part One: Hemlock

reflections on the traumas that have affected my life. I liken them here to stigmata.

STIGMATA - A CURSE FOR ORDINARY MORTALS TOO

They burrow mole-deep   these invisible imposters
ignoring the accepted parameters of
social interaction   permission unsought
I sense with trepidation their imminent visit.

Such cunning molecules   a huther of raw grief
flaking like dandruff from animal pelt
burying themselves   worm-like   in salted skin
porous with unfulfilled promises.

They excavate the epidermis   pausing awhile
to assess my reaction   cowed as I am
by past and present trauma   yet still
open to bold epiphanies.

Life's hard knocks excoriate my bones
a desert wind licking the dunes with parched tongue.

Gift or curse   they defy medical diagnosis
yet demand constant attention.

Death may halt the rampage   yet I am sceptical
for there are no certainties anymore   neither in life nor death.

First challenge - *My mother's chronic illness and death*

THE FIRST HARD KNOCK

They locked the bad news well away from me,
until death's demon croak could not be hushed.
Black bible rage became a burning bush
no one could tame, it would not let me be.
Time stolen could not ever be replaced,
sand in a timer running out too soon,
the sun eclipsed, a shadowing of the moon -
my wolf-like howl a scream through time and space.

When does a childhood end, why does the dawn
morph gold to grey when life becomes too real?
Perhaps when illness strikes, that's how we feel,
or when a mother dies, love's salve withdrawn?

Where once placenta held me tight in place,
a requiem pierced my skin and drew her face.

Second challenge - *my father's sudden demise*

DEATH AT HALLOWEEN

The second slipped down from a rainbow's back,
wrapped in raw silk, disguised as gospel truth,
deceiving me with promise of lost youth
restored, compelling me to alter tack.
My instincts faltered, self-belief was gone;
a maelstrom of confusion whirling round
within me, like a sail ship run aground
and foundered on the rocks, trust was undone.

My father   dead   ghost clutching at the wheel,
an aneurysm burst, untimely death.
No last rights, crossing of the bar unblessed,
a shipwrecked soul, his life an unfair steal.

This rainbow spun the hope all would be well,
yet left me grieving in a personal hell.

Third challenge – *coping with nyctophobia* *

ENGULFED IN DARKNESS

One moment daylight glares, I glance away,
stroll to the kitchen, put the kettle on;
returning, pause to marvel how the day
has morphed to darkness, all familiar gone.
I fear the harm that lurks beyond the door,
dark threats of violence drumming in my head...
those revenant phobias I've embraced before
bring thoughts of being strangled in my bed.

This nyctophobia has haunted me
from childhood days, I've always needed light
to shine in darkness, summoning in sleep
Ra's sun-god rays to guard me, crocus-bright.

I douse the candles – feel a strange release...
you call my name   and panic morphs to peace.

*nyctophobia – fear of the darkness

Fourth challenge – a *recurring childhood nightmare*

DROWNING

Stand still! Look how the sea is drawn to you.
Dark magnetism pulls you closer in,
and you would wade in deep in socks and shoes,
replay once more that haunting childhood scene:
a drowning man. *Act now, girl, pull him out!*
The tide turns, sweeps him back, he can't push on.
Your mother sleeps, the coastguard's on a shout,
the lifeguard clocked off early.... **You're the one!**

I was a child, afraid, too mute to scream
though storms clouds loomed, and death was imminent
Was this reality, or just a dream?
A ten-year-old the only saviour sent?

Desist! There's nothing more that could be done -
Forgiveness is superfluous   life moves on.

Fifth challenge – *the curse of having dark under-eye circles*

UGLY

They haunted me from early on, these
ink stains smeared on delicate ivory skin,
tainting the dewy blossom of my youth.

In babyhood they were there, as if someone
had used indelible ink to draw a cartoon
high on the cheekbones, christening me ugly.

Mirrors? Oh I've always hated them,
could not look myself in the eye, turned away,
hiding behind a heavy curtain fringe.

That's not the real me. I was deluded,
in public donning a shapeless ghost shroud,
a walking apology for my lack of self-belief.

I'm at fever pitch when a new ad runs
for a miracle concealer, *hides dark circles like magic!*
And I rush out, a nude-faced convert in sunglasses

to that holy of holies, the cosmetics counter,
an acolyte worshipping at the altar of Aphrodite,
hope stifling the nagging voice in my head that says
It probably won't work! And yes, I know it's hype
.

But recently I had a big aha moment, when someone
told me I had 'come-to-bed' eyes, and I whooped for joy.

Sixth challenge – *living with rheumatoid arthritis*

A LIFE-CHANGING DIAGNOSIS

My diagnosis shot a poisoned dart.
Strange symptoms, *surely nothing to be feared?*
a swollen knee, malaise that would not clear...
a tourniquet pulled tight around my heart.
Blood tests ensued, and duly summoned back
the black dog bit me ...questioned *would I live?*
I shut my ears to news they tried to give:
RA.... the room spun round, my vision black,
I almost fainted. *How would life change now?*
Limbs turned to stone, bones brittle, misaligned,
five joint replacements done, a challenging time,
patience a virtue, full recovery slow.

Remission came but damage had been done;
new knees, hips, wrist....***morphed to bionic crone!***

Seventh challenge – *loss of my best friend aged 54*

FRIENDSHIP AT CRISIS POINT

She is propped up with cushions,
a glass of lemon barley water beside her,
peppermints spilling from an open packet.
I sit on the sofa, hand her my gift.

She fumbles with the TV remote;
a huge cartoon dog is dashing
across the technicolour screen
Let me, it's tricky, I say.

I pass her the silver framed photo -
the two of us at primary school,
broad grins and NHS glasses,
all gappy teeth and optimism.

A bird crashes into the window
and she cries out.
I hug her tightly, then draw back,
shocked by her fragility...

stick arms like birds' legs,
her breath wreaking of sulphur
and disappointment....

She senses my unease.
Tears well up in her puffy eyes,
those once exquisite green jewels.

She shifts position, catches the remote.
The crazy cartoon dog barks frantically.
Shall I make tea? My voice is shaking.

She nods, attempting a weak smile.
I hurry to the kitchen, fight back tears.
Please, just keep going a little while longer

I want to keep her close   yet in my heart of hearts I know
I have to let her go.

Eighth challenge – *my Nanna's dementia*

A MAP UNLEASHES AN UNEXPECTED RESPONSE

Standing at the scullery sink   rollers in her hair,
pinafore spattered with yesterday's confusion,
she uncurls the sticky map   vintage 1914,
like a Roman general pronouncing an edict.

Squinting at the anaemic vellum she crumples.
Eternities of tears pool into the sullen creases.
She jabs with scabby finger at the centrefold.
There! Her fluted voice quivers like wind in the reed-beds.
There! Home! Let's go home!

I need to tell her she is mistaken.... yet bite my tongue,
stroke her shock of hair, grey and wiry as a clothes brush.

Her dementia is worsening.

I need to scrub the front step .... she says.

Ninth challenge – *losing the 3 people closest to me in life within 3 months*

HOPE HIDDEN IN PANDORA'S JAR

Death cast me in a roiling pool of fear,
grief, anger, trauma, chasms of despair,
these were my norm; I could not say a prayer
to Christian gods, my eyes shed pagan tears,
adopted New Age credos: colour and light,
healing with crystals, tarot, angel cards.
Old faiths denied, I wanted newer shrines
to worship at, kintsugi for lost shards.

Pandora's jar was hurled aside in rage,
smashed into smithereens, a swift reply
invoking sweet revenge, a Faustian cry
of bleak betrayal no gods could ever assuage.

Yet time brought healing, opened up the door
to projects shelved, words flowed on page once more.

Tenth challenge – *challenge of parental restrictions on my clothing choices*

HOW (NOT) TO DRESS FOR A BIRTHDAY

Blue sailor stripes reflect
my river mother's fashion taste....
a linen collar, blue-bag-starched
to a White Strand of the Monks,
sewn slant as an Emily Dickinson poem,
blue ripples iced with milky spume
cascading headlong to a roiling pool.

This quirk of sartorial elegance,
each rose-tinted birthday rushing past
in summer hopscotch disarray.
My mother's choice, a sugar-coated nod
to our seaside home; a sailor smock,
outwardly feigning bourgeois cool,
yet laced with the bohemian vibe of
her Bloomsbury alter ego.

She hated me as warrior bee
in shimmering gold and little black dress,
a scintillating belle-of-the-garden ball,
napping in campion throats,
humming a prime donna aria, yet secretly
a defrocked angel blowing a tinny trumpet
in final act of defiance...
Her sting morphed me from pampered princess
to lachrymose Cinderella in soot-black rags.

Eleventh challenge – *dissatisfaction with modern life, desire to turn the clocks back*

BECOMING EVE

Cantatas swell in my heart.
Thunderous roars from a wilderness
that shatters the marrow of fragile bones.

Harpsichord cadences float on thin air.
Déjà-vu moments finally released, threads of
lost films spooling behind closed eyelids.

I listen transfixed by the open window,
immerse myself in flashback and prolepsis.

Tides of salty tears stain the ivory keys of
my mouth,
flushing out remnants of childhood's idyll.

Time alone is precious ...
life's elixir uplifts the bruised psyche.
I brood the naked power of Eve.

For a few blissful moments
Bach's music unites us...

I am she; she is me

We are one.

Twelfth challenge – *guilt about inaction on climate change*

WHEN GAIA WEEPS

When Gaia weeps humanity trembles,
her anguished cries apocryphal.
Eye slits burst open, spew a clag of
muddy roots and salt-baked tears.

Then rain in myriad iterations -
blad, bletter, dag, driv, huther, murr,
peeggirrin, smizzle, speet or yillin*..
World's end coming,
Götterdämmerung,
no escape, no mercy.

Planet Earth seeks vengeance.
Fingers point at humankind,
that shallow vessel of inaction,
trumpeting hollow soundbites -
blame squarely placed
on shoulders hunched in denial.
The retribution will be be swift.
It is coming sooner than we think.

Gaia must not be allowed to weep.
Her Lacrimosa signifies extinction.

*words used to describe types of rainfall in the dialects of Scotland, Orkney and Shetland

Thirteenth challenge – *shock of a family member's attempted suicide, (forestalled)*

PSYCHOSIS

He is unsure how he finds himself here...
A dark night of the soul spent wrestling
with unresolved issues; an impasse,
a dawn where the familiar black dog
sinks its teeth in deeply, refusing to let go.
The rest is a blur.......

Traffic screeches to a halt...
Rubberneckers grab mobiles
in hot pursuit of the lucrative shots
destined for the tabloids.
No compassion, no consideration shown
for the wretched youngster on the parapet;
a sinister puppet,
waiting for the strings to be pulled.

Feet twitch uncontrollably,
skeleton fingers cling to the edge,
blood draining from agonised features....
All he has to do is close his eyes,
just blank out this mental torture,
this maelstrom existence and
let go! Let go forever......

Fourteenth challenge – *the longing to be a grandmother*

HOPE DENIED

Cold is the cradle where no infant sleeps,
consigned to memory's vault, yet not erased;
frame torn apart, the woodwork scuffed and grazed,
no crack through which a tiny face might peep.
A promise unfulfilled, hearts torn by grief;
hope does not spring eternal in this place;
the longed-for family sunk without a trace,
embittered words exchanged, the marriage brief.
No tinkling laughter, silence in the hall,
no toddler babbling at his mother's knee,
huge disappointment fells the family tree...
despair hangs heavy in a Payne's grey pall.

When friends show photos I must mute my screams,
fake a wry smile, choke back the broken dreams.

Fifteenth challenge – the deepest cut - *the loss of a husband*

TIME TRAVELLING WITH SKYLARKS

Remembering a concert in France, where The Lark Ascending was performed

Let's just ignore your unexpected death,
pretend it was a simple oversight,
a bad dream chased off by Aurora's light...
we were naive, too rooted to the earth.

Instead let's travel back again in time,
on skylark wings, observing avian lore,
relive our plein-air passion like before,
Vaughan William's romance echoing as we climb.

Then as the night approaches, let's alight,
rekindle memories in that cherished place –
retune to life's arpeggios, slow-paced,
hand-fasted by Selene's ethereal light.

Lying together, lovers side by side,
let's just pretend **you never really died.**

PART TWO: HONEY

Life moves on from trauma and joy slowly starts to return. These poems reflect enjoyment of nature and the seasons, festivals, travel, art, music, fashion and visits to Iona, my heart-home.

AUBADE – DUM VITA EST, SPES EST*

Dawn only half-awake,
eschewing bed-head lethargy,
reluctant adolescent peering out
from marbled sky-skein high above.

Her features emulate a theatre backdrop,
Curlicues blushing pink in embryonic bloom,
a serendipitous bouquet harvested from nocturnal fantasies.

Soon she will unleash her winnowed locks,
her radiance casting spells on flora, fauna, biota.
Today is vernal coronation day.

*dum vita est, spes est – while there is life there is hope

LIFE'S NATURAL RHYTHMS

Above our heads a raft of pulsing cloud
blown in on gentle zephyrs from the west;
sign of Ostara's gold, her eager quest
to sow her seeds of life on fertile ground
Each sunrise boasts a naked golden glow
expanding in dimension hour by hour,
until the sky morphs under Zephyros' power
to midday bliss, life's pulse in rapturous flow.
Then later, cumulus clouds amass together
like sheep when herded tightly in a fold,
purled tight to keep them snug against the cold;
an augury of changes to the weather.

Red sky at night, portent of morning glory.
Red sky at dawn, beware, a different story.

EXPECT THE UNEXPECTED

Reflections on the changing nature of the seasons

Late hoar-frost breaks the brittle bones of morning,
the lawn still dressed in silver-laced chemise,

teasing a desire for nights by dog grate embers;
taunting ears too eager to catch the blackbird's first

notes of primrose song; those shy spectral arpeggios
drifting from distant orchards on thin ghost-breath.

Why this deceit, this plot to unfoot the unwary;
a random game of seasonal musical chairs?

Our bio clocks tick tock like metronomes,
heartbeats observe the iambic pentameter of life;

a place where the pendulum swing is regular, confident,
where seasonal flow brings comfort -

>   but not this year!

HIDE AND SEEK *(a metaphor for life's thrills and spills)*

Clicking the stiff latch   sliding lizard-bellied
into a night black as a stream of spilt molasses
we slide our way over goose-wing gravel chips,
tongues taut as William Tell's arrow behind
battlements of moon-shimmer teeth.

Nearby an owl   reckless in down-swoop
sets yew twigs cracking in brisk staccato

Light in a window   sudden   secretive   suspicious...
The hunters conniving   capture and ridicule looming

Warily we hedgehog-curl   roll into the
lee side of taxus baccata's mothering arms -

find welcome Sanctuary!

SUMMER'S LAST DANCE

Spent coils of sunlight dreaming of *Swan Lake*;
ochre, copper, alizarin crimson tutus, fading mosaics

of wilted glory, shrivelled leaves still perfecting *sautés*,
pliés,, jetés...... veteran ballerinas at the *barre*.

Deciduous trees spin in defiant last waltz;
once gaudy boughs shimmy to earth's steady drumbeat.

Late summer breezes join the revelry, whipping leaves
into spirals, luring them into frenzied *tarantellas*.

A fieldworker looks on, beats time, his spade splitting
the clay with the relatable *shuff shuff* of a proud djembe.

Then tears come streaming free   as the curtain falls and
a Judas tree bends low in *arabesque* over summer's mouldering grave.

RIVER MOTHER

River mother sings
to the crooked quercus,
to windswept fields,
burnished with toppled corn bales,
ululates the seductive hum
of pagan summers.

She whispers to
penumbras of wood sprites,
to star watchmen blowing
on frozen fingers,
murmurs to the wastelands
of ice-barbed winters.

Life-giver, life-taker,
sustainer of the foetus in the womb,
transporter of dead souls across the bar
propulgator of flora and fauna,
rewilder of abandoned spaces,
her credentials impeccable.

She is a wise crone
mirroring our *humanitas*,
tracing pilgrims from cradle to grave;
between source and delta
an instinctive ritual,
playing out from vaults of deep time.

EVENING ON THE NORFOLK COAST

Sea-shell hearts languishing on pine-fringed beaches
Shallow water in the creek   sickle of sallow moonbeams

Footsteps aching to turn again for home   dreaming of
winding back the years   unencumbered   to childhood's zenith

A seagull settles   angel wings outspread on a boulder
We stumble on silently   navigate seaweed breakwaters

Daylight is shrinking fast   time to retreat before high tide -
rivulets already snake around mudbanks, a trap for the unwary

Climbing the slipway steps we turn   glimpse advent candles
in beach hut windows   a twinkle of hope in midwinter chill.

We are between dog and wolf

      tastes of childhood rising in teacup hearts

         Tonight we will drink from life's chalice

            whisper an *ave* for humanity's feral soul.

THIS IS ENOUGH FOR ME ....

My artist's bed still warm with oversleeping

Life's palette drizzling autumn's blossoming grace;

splashes of ochre, umber, carmine, sepia

rippling mosaics on watermelon sheets ...

chiaroscuro for my thirsty soul.

MONET PURSUES HIS OBSESSION WITH WATER LILIES

Heat haze lingers,
shadows glide ghost-like across a meadow-green morning;

A cast of nubile nymphs
seated by the pond, teasing stubborn knots from luscious locks.

I observe the dancers
in Pierrot costumes, rehearsing for a private matinée,

tuning in to the whisper of
feather-light ripples; gentle sonatas rippling through reed-beds;

I hear the call of starlings
aligning in murmuration to sweep across a sherbet-pink sky.

I reflect that surely someone
should capture this rich tapestry, this glimpse of a May morning Eden?

Behind leaf-green shutters
the ghost of first wife Camille stirs...but she will not leave her sanctuary.

As I linger on the wooden bridge,
I'm certain this is exactly how the great man himself must have observed it;

a theatrical cast of lilies,
a life's work to commit to canvas in painterly detail for posterity.

Although half-blind,
the master takes canvas, brush, paint and easel. This is his Nirvana.

Eh voilà! Les Nymphéas.

ZOOMORPHIC* TALISMAN

My silver ring serves well as talisman,
exquisite in its craft, portraying skill
of artisans, whose progeny are still
at work today, here on Iona's isle.
Hand-made with love from Dalriada's* land;
the wearing of it brings a secret thrill.

It fits the slim fourth finger of my hand,
adorns it with zoomorphic patterning,
depicting Celtic beasts, whose symbols bring
an insight of past times and ancient lore..
I picture Druid priests in prayer, who stand
in woodland groves where trees spread guardian wings.

The Celts handcrafted sacred jewellery
to nurture souls wherever they might dwell;
traced back in history to the Book of Kells,
revered as being honed by angel hands;
delightful motifs with strong symmetry,
guarding the noble class with powerful spells.

The silver metal used drew on the moon,
whose healing powers we value still today;
a talisman when walking Columb's* way,
fecundity that nurtures plants and seeds:
I wear my ring, trust that her power will
protect me always, steer good luck my way.

*Zoomorphic - carefully curated silver jewellery is made at the Celtic heritage gallery, Aosdana, on the island of Iona. Some pieces are patterned with abstract animal forms, known as zoomorphic patterns.

*Dalriada - a former Gaelic kingdom (5th century ad -9th century ad) comprising Argyll, parts of the Inner Hebrides, and parts of modern Antrim.

*Columb - Saint Columba

A HOPELESS FASHION ADDICT REFLECTS ON RECYCLING

I often wonder if they feel sad,
the recycled clothes in the charity shop?
Maybe they feel rejected? Suffer separation anxiety?
I imagine them holding parties in the wardrobe
when their owners are out at work,
getting high on moth balls, swinging naked on coat hangers,
shoes shamelessly tapping out the Charleston in their racks.
Those Jimmy Choos, what an incredible Oxfam find!
Too small for my feet..... but I love them anyway.
I like to coax them out of their box and stroke them
as you stroke a cat, hold them to my ear and
hear them purr. I stare into their lacquered reflection
and see my face ..... a lopsided moon, squidgy,
out of focus as in a fairground hall of mirrors.
Was she an arrogant rich bitch, their first owner?
Or a regular nine-to-five shopgirl who won the lottery?
What stories those shoes could tell if only they had
the power of speech.
I could listen all day!

THE COMFORTING RITUALS OF LIFE IN A SMALL COUNTRY VILLAGE

Notes to self on observing a village funeral

The village street is teeming with black crows, wings spread wide as they hop and step with an odd gait towards the church. The bells are tolling slowly, solemnly, as is fitting, yet observing from the upstairs window I now see that in reality they are not crows but people. The men wear Trilby hats, firmly perched on serious heads, bodies swathed in dark woollen coats, collars up against the sharp slap of the winter gale. They hold hands in a protective way with their womenfolk, dressed a little more boldly with tweed skirts flipping out from beneath black capes, a jaunty feather flying from a grey hat or a tartan shawl poking out, escaping from around a dowager's neck. They surge, like the current of a flooding river - heads down, intent only on arriving at the church before the cortège. It could be a portrait from a pre-war era, when villagers en masse would march along to church in crocodile formation, eager to pay their last respects to the deceased, be he high -ranking or lowly in status. It mattered not, death was, (is), a leveller, a unifier. We can't escape it. There is maybe a soupçon of *schadenfreude* behind the grim faces: *Thank God it's not me !* Yes, we are all guilty of that. Flushed cheeks belie the relief; *not me, not yet!* Observing the scene, I feel I have no right to be here. Am I just a peeping Tom, up to no good? With irreverent haste I whip the net curtain across, bob as I quickly cross myself at an imaginary altar and recite an Ave Maria.... for good luck...just in case.

AN UNEXPECTED VISITATION *Celebrating the joy of Christmas and its traditions*

Christmas Night   a tap tap at the Manor door,
startled revellers in froufrou and greasepaint
pause their masquerade:

the eponymous Harlequin, Pantalone, Pierrot, Columbina
and Capitano   mouse-still now   fingers to lips
.
Through the latticed oriole a blinding radiance,
lux aeterna   a new beginning,
celestial music shakes the palladium.

Lord Christmas strides ogre-like to the door,

     confronts a barefoot ragamuffin child,

          eyes entreating seasonal charity

Gentle as a snowflake   he scoops her up,
creates a warm bed in the inglenook's feathered womb.

HEMLOCK AND HONEY

On visiting the Elgar Museum and hearing his music again

We cross the museum threshold
almost on tiptoe, conversation withheld.

Those soothing strains, a quiet confidence,
violins soaring like birds in summer flight.

Then a sudden sharp intake of breath;
that familiar score on the music stand;

Salut d'amour, Love's Greeting, transporting me
back twenty-six years in a whirl of hemlock and honey;

bittersweet nectar for a soul emerging from the shadows
of loss, cautiously stepping out along a new path...

And in the orchard he's there again, reclining on a bench,
lost in the moment, his cane propped up beside him,

head nodding in time to the rise and fall of the
music's bold cadences. My mood lifts, negativity now

subtly altered by this serendipitous moment ....
What rapture! And suddenly....

I marvel that my mouth can smile again
a wide, beaming, upturned-corners smile.

This..... yes this, right now, is my long-awaited epiphany.

ACKNOWLEDGMENT

I would like to express my thanks to poet Anna Saunders for her invaluable workshops on writing sonnets, which provided the inspiration for many of the poems in this book

Becoming Eve was long listed for the Gloucestershire Poetry Open Poetry Prize and was first published in the magazine Gloucestershire Open Poetry Competition anthology 2023

First versions of *Friendship at Crisis Point* and *Psychosis* appeared in April Skies anthology from Hedgehog Poetry Press

First version of *Notes to self on observing a village funeral* and *expect the Unexpected* appeared in various Flights' e-Journals from flightofthedragonfly.com

River Mother and *Drowning* appeared in an anthology from Yaffle Press entitled What *we inherit from water in Spring 2025*

Finally, I am indebted to the former editor of *Impspired Magazine,* Steve Cawte, for believing in my poetry and agreeing to publish this pamphlet. He was a great supporter of my poetry but sadly passed away August 2024 before publication could take place.

A map unleashes an unexpected response and This is enough for me first appeared in *Erbacce* Journal Autumn 2024

However, I am equally indebted to Mark Davidson of *Hedgehog Poetry Press* for agreeing to take over publication of this pamphlet.

www.ingramcontent.com/pod-product-compliance
Lightning Source LLC
Chambersburg PA
CBHW021639080526
44584CB00015BA/1615